Dear Refugee

Dear Refugee

Amir Darwish

Smokestack Books
1 Lake Terrace, Grewelthorpe, Ripon HG4 3BU
e-mail: info@smokestack-books.co.uk
www.smokestack-books.co.uk

ISBN 978-1-9996742-2-9

Smokestack Books
is represented
by Inpress Ltd

To my wife,
Shareen

Contents

Dear refugee

Be thankful to the roads,
Their stones as they lie before you
To the sky that generously shows you
The moon dangling its legs in your eyes,
Say thank you to nature, to the rivers who feed
The earth to feed you,
Be thankful to life and earth
When they knock open your heart.

We want to live

On the margin of a forgotten camp
We want to live with pain
With sadness
With agony
With trauma
We want to live
With or without food
We want to live
With thirst
With enemies or without them
We still want to live
Under a torn tent leaking rain at night we want to live
We want to live
At the long queues for clothes we want to live
With every step we take towards death
We want to live
With every tree we pass
With every pride swallowed, we want to live
With or without our children
We want to live
With or without our parents
We want to live
We want to live
Bcause we love life.

Where I come from

From the earth I come
From the heart of Africa
From the kidneys of Asia
From India with its spices I come
From a deep Amazonian forest
From a Tibetan meadow I come
From an ivory land
From far away
From everywhere around me
From where there are trees, mountains, rivers and seas
From here, there and everywhere
From the womb of the Mediterranean I come
From a mental scar
From closed borders
From a camp with a thousand tents
From a bullet wound
From the face of a lonely child
From a single mother's sigh
From a hole in an inflatable boat about to sink
From a bottle of water for fifty to share
From frozen snot in a toddler's nose
From the tear on a father's cheek
From a hungry stomach
From a graffiti that reads, 'I was here once'
From a missing limb
Like a human I come to share the space.

What I left behind

I left that table with three books, a tea glass dirty
An ashtray
The TV remote still lost somewhere between cushions

A wall with a mixture of rotten green broken yellow light
A small window into an empty street
A lonely white tissue blowing in a ruined alley

I left a pregnant apple tree
A sink full of pans from last night's meal
My plate among them with a tulip

I left half a bottle of red wine near the bed
Money notes wrinkled
A belt with broken buckle

The painting in the corridor
The tearful man in it has his hand on his cheek
The forest behind him is as huge as the memory it left behind

I left a tape-recorder a lover once gave me
Playing the Kurdish singer Mohammed Sixo
Singing 'Oh the land Oh the land'

I left my school desk engraved with my name
The teacher who lectured me every time I brought a poetry book
To school instead of my homework

I left the old corner shop
Containing a debt book
That has my name in it

I left a pair of new shoes
The yellow laces I bought
To go with them

I left my mother who used to call me when it was time to eat
I left a generous father who used to bring home bags of figs, apples
And occasionally a roast chicken

I left home.

The news has just arrived

The news has just arrived
That the red wine bottle is still in its place
Unmoved,
Untouched
Half empty.

Near it there is a broken window
An open door and a woman crying by the corner
The liquid inside the bottle rattles every time
A tear falls then it settles again
The dust of falling buildings
Has covered the full half.

And I am here
I can no longer lift the bottle up
And look to see how thick the wine is
Or what I can see through it.
Nonetheless, the news has just arrived
That my wine bottle still stands.

I will write

I will write of birds, streams, trees and clouds
Of a husband who places a peck on his wife's forehead
Of the dry rose in a book of love poems
Of the lover who writes *habiby* on a pine tree in a park
Of a girl who smells jasmine on her way to school
I will write of her as she runs barefoot
Then pops her blisters at night
I will write of the song she hears in her head when she wakes
Of the neighbour who calls in for coffee
And leaves secret love letters under her pillow
I will wrote of picnics, melons swimming in water,
I will write of solitude and its thirty-six children.

Fizzy drink

Once near a
Grocery store,
I bought a fizzy drink
Then shook it.

Twenty years later,
I gaze into that bottle
On a window sill
Here.

Afraid to
Lift the lid,
And acknowledge
The taste.

Come what may,
I will open
The bottle
One day.

I am an immigrant and I love life

I love the leaf that falls in spring
The peck on a toddler's cheek before nursery
The water as it steams in the bathroom
The remnants of hair in the shower
I love life
The full moon in your eyes
The sun filling my own
I love the roads like a network of veins
I am an immigrant and I love life.

If I ever see love

If I ever see love wondering alone,
I will take it in,
Make my heart its home
And my eyes its window to the world.
I will keep it there forever
And ever
And ever.

We are in love

I love you like the day in the young dawn
My arms embrace the sun in your eyes
Saying goodbye to darkness.
Humble, simple and systematic
My heart beats as the day gets stronger,
While my eyes freeze around your waist.
Dusk strikes and so do our lips.
Lickable as honey, our thoughts furnish the land with desire.

Have I done enough to love you?

I have turned this entire body into a tear to fall for you.
I have nothing in this heart but a home for you.
I have a pool of wine in these kidneys.
So drink.
I have the Mediterranean in this liver.
I have you sail across it daily.
I have closed every poetic line with a syllable that looks like you.
I have opened another with your eyelash.
I have loved you like the sun has loved the earth since creation,
Not a day passes when they do not see each other.
I have pens in these bones to write your name as I walk.
I have managed to fit you with all the roses of the world in sole heart.
I have rewritten the entire history of love for you.
I have even loved those who hate you, just because they think of you.
I have left a pen near my gravestone,
So write and tell me if I have done enough to love you.

This heart

This heart is a house.
Love knocks at the door
Comes in
And sits on the floor
Looks out the window
And see lovers pass weeping.

Poetry and me

Deep in a forest
I see a stream,
Poetry sits
On the bank.

I sit down
And put a hand
Across its shoulder
And say:

Never have I felt at home
Like here,
Next to you
I can see every detail in life.

Poetry replies:
My heart is big enough
For everyone
To swim in this stream.

I listen to the water flow inside me.
I am also at home like this
Happy with who
I am.

Take my heart

My dearest, take my heart,
Take it since it's you who owns it
Nurture it as you go along,
Because it longer beats as it should.
Talk to it gently and cool its passion.
The finest moment, my darling, is when
My heart divides itself: half mine, half yours.

Kurdistan

Uneven earth, roaring trees
Childlike water and fashionably late thoughts.
Land of no-one open its arms and take the earth in.
Flatter the symptoms of joy
Gone with the wind
And push open the window
To breath in the perfume of pomegranates, olives and love.

The Shade

The shade is balm to my eyes
The blinding sun sends honeyed arrows of love
Like feathers illuminating the steps.
I walk on wine and sink into burns.
Scars decorate the entrance
To a stone heart and a door made of pearls.
Hairs fall on a bed
The air is free.
You can give up the world
But the world never gives up on you.

My place

It's cold and raining in your heart.
Where do I go now?
My only home is here.
I am scared to leave it.
I worry that another lover will come in and take my place,
Sit next to the fire,
Lay his head on his folded hands and fall asleep.
I will never leave.
As cold as it feels
Your love is still inside me
Boiling like lava in my arteries.

It's a mistake to think love ends

It's a mistake to think love ends.
Love is the bud of the bud,
The rose of the rose,
The soul inside the soul of the clear sky.
There.
Right there.
During the day it is blinding like the sun
At night it's a moon in the shadow of a mountain
And that old café in the corner of your eye...
Two chairs, a table, a glass, the two of us, one heart, one beat.
It's a mistake to think love ends,
That it dies like the nerve-end of a finger trapped in a door.
It's a mistake to think love ends.
A greasy house, laughter.
A leaf, a tree.
It is a mistake to think love ends.
A mistake. A mistake. A mistake.
7am.
A single bed.
One pillow (stuffed with wool).
A colourful sheet.

Close love

Chemicals move
When lovers kiss
Hands find their way around the body
Eyes shut themselves slowly
Throats swallow love thoughts.
Love is always closer than you think.

Dear love

I got your postcard.
'Sorry, I am no longer with you
Kind regards,
Love.'

Fine, let see if you can manage
Without sneaking into my bed at night
Whispering, 'let's make love'.
Can you really give up gazing out of the window
As the moon disappears into our eyes?
How did you arrive at this decision?
Were you drunk when you wrote this postcard?
Gone are the days when Mozart sent you to sleep in my arms.
Gone is the time you flew into my heart to shelter in winter,
Beside the warm fire of my thoughts.

I must look love in the eye

I must look love in the eye and tell it the story
Of two new lovers,
Their netted hands holding one another,
I see them walking under the crescent moon,
Swinging and jumping into an ocean of lilies.
They swim against the entire universe,
Change its behaviour
Habits,
Customs,
Cultures,
Religions.
They make humans more human
Become lovers forever.

I once loved a girl

I once loved a girl
Who gave herself to me beneath a hill.
I laughed and asked:
Will you marry me?
Ask for my hand, said she.
Of whom? said I.
My parents, said she.
Where are they? said I.
Far away, said she.
Let's go, said I.
Now? said she.
Yes, said I.

When my beloved appears

My beloved breaks into my room at night,
She sits at the foot of my bed and sighs.
She runs her hand through the lilacs in her hair.
Love passes by the window on a breeze.
She puts a finger to her lips,
'Hush' she whispers, 'hush... don't speak.
Let go of everything,
Come close, so close, and live here inside me.'
My beloved is hungry
She invites herself to eat from a banquet
Of trance-like devotion, passion and roses.

When a shadow enters a shadow, a lover appears in between,
Walks with the moon and goes close to its heart,
It is difficult to tell them apart.
When love appears on a mountain peak,
Near a lonely rose, it releases a sigh,
Blinks an eye to swallow the moon,
Relaxes deep into a trance.
When a lover appears suddenly in your life,
You can do nothing but surrender.

Words to a lover

Lover...
Through the window comes a full moon.
In the middle there is a rose with five red petals.
The stars are clear.
The branch of a pine tree comes between us.
The shadow of a man crosses the pavement.
A lover comes close, so close,
Rests her chin on my shoulder,
Fastens her arms around my heart and silently sighs.
She takes my heart in exchange for the moon.

The lemon you once gave me
Is still here in my pocket.

Star

A star shone on the path
We walked,
The path we walk and will always be walking.
The reflection of its shining eyes
Cracks Efrini's walnut trees.
And the star's gaze,
Oh it lit the way
Through a Kurdish olive grove
That changed our hearts from
Sense to senseless
In the land of dismay.
Today *Shareen* was born.

Daily routine

I wake up everyday
Pair my thoughts together
Like I do when I put my black socks together after a wash
They are all the same colour
But there have to be picked carefully.
Not all dark colours are the same.

Just saw a moon

I just saw a moon, half shy, half out.
Its light is still in my eyes.
The figure zigzags away in front of me.
Oh, I am in trance, a trance.

I speak of Teesside

Of the big giant chimneys that pump air, life, and laughter
Into the sky in the shape of big muscled steel man.

Of the sky and its birds as they fly high and low,
Making noise in circles while children watch, point and scream.

Of Osmotherley and the homemade honey
That found its way to my heart.

Of Teesside Park on Thursday nights,
Beautiful as a Middle Eastern bride
Waiting for her groom by the candle light.

I speak of Victoria Road as it feasts on Eid
And the students walking home from the library.

Morning of tulips

It is a morning of tulips.
Ones that open with your eyes
And stay awake forever.
My dear, every morning there are new tulips
Come alive at your awakening.
Good morning to my *habiby*,
I am coming to collect you soon.

Stone

I watched a rolling stone
Drop from the heights of a castle
Into the swimming pool of your eyes.
It's the same stone
I kicked while surfing
The skin of your body
And watched closely
As it landed here, in my kidneys.

There it bounced up to reach
The unknown mountain
Whose peak we want to climb.
Sad and lonely,
It stayed there
Until you forced it into my mouth
Where it fell into my heart.

Now my heart is made of stone.

Toilet

There is a tile on the right hand side
There is an exotic art picture on the wall
There is comfort in looking at it
There is a man in that picture embracing a lover
There is consistency in everything around here
There is nowhere like this
No other place where we are so equal.

Perfectly

Last night the moon shied away.
But the sun is out and waving today.

Hailstones

So white, circular
Identical to each other
In weight and temperature.
Perfectly shaped
They live for just a few minutes.
They speak the language of those they fall on,
Utter the sadness of every human they touch,
Sliding slowly down your face, leaving scars as souvenirs.

Tonight is the night

When a blade will make its way across my veins
Like a toddler walking gingerly
When a rope will be tight around my neck like a lover saying goodbye
When the tablets will fill my stomach and rattle like two Middle
Eastern tribes swallowed by a whale and continuing their blood feud
in its belly
When the train will scatter my body into a million pieces like a ton of
cherry tomatoes let loose from a mountain peak.
Where a fall from the tenth floor will turn my bones into salt
And a jump from a bridge will flush my body like a ten-year-old
intact kidney stone
When my head in the oven will burn, burn, burn, until nothing is left
but ashes, or until my brain becomes a tiny piece of charcoal
When a bullet will dig deep into my heart like an endless dark well.

Tonight is the night to give up everything that matters and that does
not matter
Tonight I will masturbate for the last time with you in mind
I will not think of all the fertile sperm I left behind
I will be free from everything and nothing
Free from agony, pain, embarrassment, funny memories
From the stain of all lovers on my body
Free from freedom itself
Free from the ifs and buts and dos and don'ts
Free like never before
When contemplation of you will end at long last
When my breath will stop
Tonight I will shout free at last, free at last,
Thanks to all those who know me I am free at last.

If you are British I am British too

If you are British I am British too
I sleep every night just like you do
I find myself in situations I never knew
I sniff the same air as you
I travel by plane, train and car
Where the language is concerned I also don't have a clue
I eat fish and chips too
I go to the shop to buy bread and milk to see my hunger through
If you are British I am British too
I eat with my mouth
And go to the loo
I bleed the same colour as you
I get sick just like you
I drink coffee and tea and I take milk too
If you are British I am British too
I walk the dog when he wants me to
I see the birds fly in the same sky as you.

If you took time to walk in my shoe
You will see that if I am British you are British too
I am American, Syrian, Bangladeshi, Colombian, Indian,
Pakistani, South African, Polish, Brazilian, Korean, Chinese,
I am white, black and pink
But above all I am human like you
If you are British I am British too.